DATE DUE

15.98

STECK-VAUGHN

PORTRAIT OF AMERICA

Hawaii

Steck-Vaughn Company

Executive Editor	Diane Sharpe
Senior Editor	Martin S. Saiewitz
Design Manager	Pamela Heaney
Photo Editor	Margie Foster

Proof Positive/Farrowlyne Associates, Inc.
Program Editorial, Revision Development, Design, and Production

Reviewer: Hawaii Visitors Bureau

Published by Raintree Steck-Vaughn Publishers, an imprint of Steck-Vaughn Company.

A Turner Educational Services, Inc. book. Based on the Portrait of America television series by R. E. (Ted) Turner.

Cover Photo: Cover photography of waterfalls by © Comstock.

Library of Congress Cataloging-in-Publication Data

Thompson, Kathleen.
   Hawaii / Kathleen Thompson.
      p.   cm. — (Portrait of America)
   "Based on the Portrait of America television series" — T.p.   verso.
   "A Turner book."
   Includes index.
   ISBN 0-8114-7331-7 (library binding).
   ISBN 0-8114-7438-4 (softcover).
      1. Hawaii—Juvenile literature. I. Portrait of America (Television program) II. Title.
III. Series: Thompson, Kathleen. Portrait of America.
DU623.26.T57 1996
996.9—dc20   95-35822
                                                    CIP
                                                    AC

Printed and Bound in the United States of America

1 2 3 4 5 6 7 8 9 10 WZ 98 97 96 95

Acknowledgments
The publishers wish to thank the following for permission to reproduce photographs:
P. 7 Waimea Convention & Visitors Bureau; p. 8 © Ann Cecil/Stock Photos Hawaii; p. 10 Waimea Convention & Visitors Bureau; pp. 11, 12, 13, 14 Bishop Museum; p. 15 North Wind Picture Archives; p. 16 Bishop Museum; p. 17 The Bettmann Archive; p. 18 Bishop Museum; p. 19 US Senate; pp. 20, 21, 22, 23 Bishop Museum; p. 24 Waimea Convention & Visitors Bureau; p. 26 © Photri; p. 27 (both) © Camera Hawaii, Inc.; p. 28 (top) © Current Events, (bottom) © Peter French/Stock Photos Hawaii; p. 29 (top) Hawaii Department of Land & Natural Resources, (bottom) © Current Events; pp. 30, 31 (both) Courtesy Bob Kiger; pp. 32, 33 Courtesy Michael Faye; pp. 34, 36 © Camera Hawaii, Inc.; p. 37 © Ann Cecil/Stock Photos Hawaii; p. 38 © J. Castle/Stock Photos Hawaii; p. 39 © Scott Lopez/Hawaii Volcanoes National Park; p. 41 © George Theofanis/Stock Photos Hawaii; pp. 42, 44 Waimea Convention & Visitors Bureau; p. 46 One Mile Up; p. 47 (left) One Mile Up, (center, right) Hawaii Visitors Bureau.

STECK-VAUGHN

PORTRAIT OF AMERICA

Hawaii

Kathleen Thompson

A Turner Book

RSVP

RAINTREE
STECK-VAUGHN
PUBLISHERS
The Steck-Vaughn Company

Austin, Texas

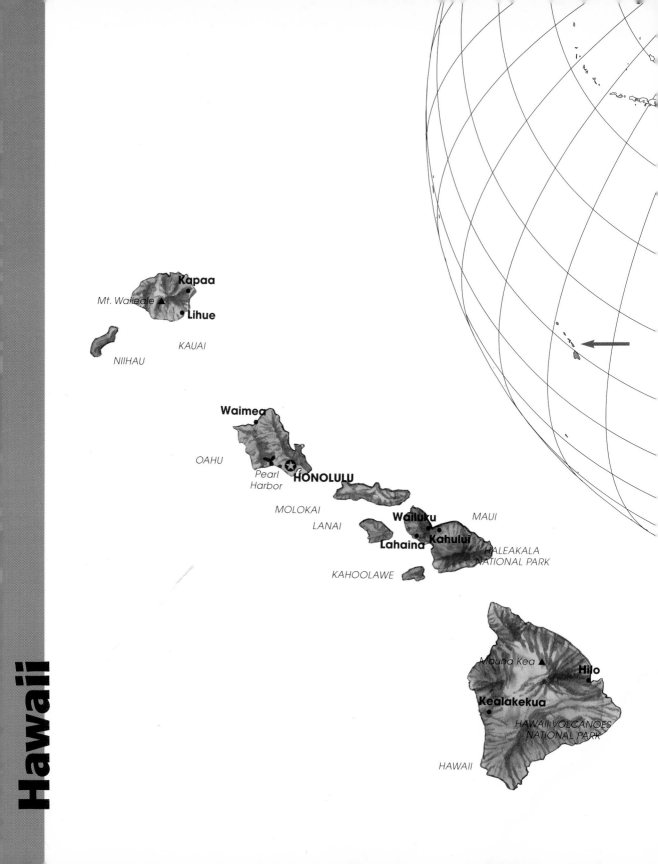

Hawaii

Kapaa

Mt. Waileale ▲

Lihue

KAUAI

NIIHAU

Waimea

OAHU

Pearl
Harbor

HONOLULU

MOLOKAI

LANAI

Wailuku

MAUI

Lahaina

Kahului

HALEAKALA
NATIONAL PARK

KAHOOLAWE

Mauna Kea ▲

Hilo

Kealakekua

HAWAII VOLCANOES
NATIONAL PARK

HAWAII

Contents

Introduction

All of Hawaii came from somewhere else—its people, animals, plants, even the land itself. The islands welled up as volcanoes from far beneath the ocean—barren and isolated. Yet life eventually found them. Seeds, borne on currents of wind and water, took hold first. Then, insects and birds found their way to the islands. Humans came much later—voyagers from the south in great seagoing canoes. They brought pigs and taro plants, skills, customs, and their belief in powerful gods to sustain their life. Later still, Europeans, Americans, and Asians found—and almost lost—this paradise. They mingled, jostled, and clashed with one another and with the islanders. The result was a lively, many-layered culture, completely Hawaiian, like no other on Earth.

A couple looks out at the colorful rock walls at Waimea Canyon on the island of Kauai.

Hawaii

Islands Out of the Sea

For millions of years, lava has poured up out of underwater volcanoes, building and shaping islands in the middle of the Pacific Ocean. One hundred and thirty-two of them form the chain of islands we call Hawaii. Until about 1,200 years ago, no one lived on the islands. Between A.D. 400 and 900, Polynesians from the Marquesas Islands and Tahiti settled some of the Hawaiian Islands. These people were excellent navigators and boat makers. The Polynesians had no written language. Their culture was rich in myths and legends, which were passed along by oral tradition. Their religion was based on a belief in gods existing in all forms. These people had a powerful ruling class, called the *alii nui*. A taboo system, called *kapu*, provided rules for maintaining the political and social order.

A British explorer, Captain James Cook, landed at present-day Waimea, on Kauai, on January 20, 1778. He named the land the Sandwich Islands in honor of the Earl of Sandwich, who was the head of the British

This statue of King Kamehameha I is decorated with leis on Kamehameha Day. King Kamehameha founded the kingdom of Hawaii.

9

The coastline of the island of Kauai is where Captain James Cook first landed.

Navy. On a return voyage the following year, Cook and the Hawaiians argued over a boat that was missing or stolen. Cook and several of his men were killed by the Hawaiians at Kealakekua on February 14, 1779.

For some time after that, Europeans left the islands alone. But Hawaii's position as a way station between Asia and America was too attractive. Eventually trading ships began stopping regularly. The Europeans were interested in Hawaiian sandalwood, which they traded in China. With the traders came Protestant missionaries who taught the Hawaiians about Christianity. The traders also brought with them many infectious diseases that the islanders could not fend off. At this time, Hawaii had about three hundred thousand people. But this number steadily declined throughout the first half of the century as the diseases took their toll.

The islands were not politically united in the eighteenth century. There were smaller units of government, sometimes covering a single island, sometimes including several islands. Kamehameha I gained control of Hawaii in a war that lasted ten years, 1782–1792. He used European firearms, which he acquired from foreign merchants. By 1810 he controlled all of the remaining islands. Kamehameha I

During his three voyages, Captain James Cook explored many places, including Hawaii, Tahiti, New Zealand, Australia, and Antarctica.

Kamehameha I united all of the Hawaiian Islands under his rule.

set up his own governors to rule the individual islands. He took control of all trade. Kamehameha I died in 1819. One year later his son Liholiho, who ruled Hawaii as Kamehameha II, brought about the collapse of many of the old rituals. He also abolished the Hawaiian religions. Soon after, he embraced the religion of the Protestant missionaries.

The missionaries influenced the culture of the people. They taught the islanders how to write and other skills. Soon there were schools, churches, frame houses, and general stores. What's more, the missionaries became advisers to the government. When Kamehameha III became the ruler in 1825, change continued at the same pace. In 1835 the first permanent sugar plantation went into operation. It was owned by an American group of business leaders.

Kamehameha III was responsible for laying down the foundations of constitutional government in Hawaii. The Declaration of Rights and the Edict of Toleration were written in 1839. A written constitution was added a year later. These documents had many of the characteristics of the United States Constitution, including personal rights. The constitution allowed for a new structure of government, with executive, legislative, and judicial branches.

Meanwhile, sugar plantations and other industries developed in Hawaii. The island's population was not large enough to support these industries. Owners had to bring in workers from other countries. The first to arrive were the Chinese. By the mid-1860s, there were more Chinese on the islands than Europeans. In 1875 King Kalakaua signed a treaty with the United States that opened up the sugar cane trade even more. The plantations brought in additional workers from Japan, the Philippines, Korea, Portugal, and Puerto Rico.

As the plantation owners and other business leaders became more and more powerful, they came in conflict with the government. Many of these business leaders were Americans, whose interest in the island

This picture shows an early nineteenth century missionary preaching to the islanders.

was strictly to make money. In 1887 a group of business leaders led a revolution against King Kalakaua. They forced him to accept a new constitution in which the king had little or no power. The power was now in the hands of the mostly foreign-born business leaders. These people established the Reform party, which began to work closely with the United States. They began to push toward making Hawaii a part of the United States.

In 1891 King Kalakaua died. His sister, Liliuokalani, became queen. She was determined to regain power for the monarchy and for the Hawaiian people. She tried to get rid of the constitution put in place by the Reform party and create a new one. Her efforts were stopped by a revolution that was supported by the United States ambassador to Hawaii, John L. Stevens. Stevens did not have permission from the United States government. When American troops stationed at Honolulu supported the revolution, Queen Liliuokalani surrendered. She expressed the hope that the United States Congress would not approve of the support Stevens had given to the revolution.

The revolutionaries immediately tried to get the United States to take over Hawaii. President Grover Cleveland ordered an investigation, which

Queen Liliuokalani was the last in a line of Hawaiian monarchs that began with Kamehameha I.

showed that the revolution would not have succeeded without Stevens's help. He ordered that the monarchy be restored. The revolutionaries refused, however. Instead, they set up their own government and also appointed businessowner Sanford B. Dole president. Queen Liliuokalani and her followers tried a counter-revolution in 1895, but they did not have the forces to succeed. On January 24, 1895, the queen agreed to sign a formal surrender in order to win pardons for her supporters who had been jailed.

United States business interests now controlled the affairs on the islands. On August 12, 1898, the

On June 14, 1900, Sanford Dole was inaugurated governor of the Territory of Hawaii.

This is how the Olowalu Sugar Mill looked between 1870 and 1890. Although less sugar cane is grown now, it is still Hawaii's most important crop.

United States annexed Hawaii. Two years later Hawaii was no longer an independent country but became a territory of the United States. Sanford B. Dole was appointed governor.

The population of Hawaii at the turn of the century had declined to about 154,000 people. Native Hawaiians were becoming a smaller and smaller part of the population. The production of both pineapples and sugar cane was growing rapidly. Both of these crops were controlled by only a few large companies. In 1911 the United States constructed a major naval port, Pearl Harbor. Other large military bases were also built.

By 1920 people started to talk about statehood for Hawaii. Because Hawaii was a territory of the United

States, its citizens had to pay taxes to the federal government. They did not have a voice in Congress, however. This taxation without representation should have been a familiar tune to United States political figures. It was one of the issues American colonists tried to resolve with Great Britain prior to the American Revolution.

On December 7, 1941, Japanese forces attacked Pearl Harbor and airfields on Oahu. Now the United

More than two thousand people were killed in Japan's attack on Pearl Harbor. President Roosevelt called December 7, 1941, "a day which will live in infamy."

States was at war with Japan. Hawaii was placed under martial law. A curfew was enforced. The military took over the courts and law enforcement. The United States government doubted the loyalty of the *nisei*—Americans of Japanese descent. In California, the nisei were put in detention camps. In Hawaii, there were too many Japanese Americans to do that.

The 100th Battalion was a volunteer group of nisei soldiers who fought for the United States in Europe. Through their bravery, they became the most decorated unit in the United States Armed Forces. Many members of this battalion came back to Hawaii and formed the center of a group that challenged the

This girl's face reflects the happiness many Hawaiians felt when Hawaii became the fiftieth state.

political power in the islands after the war. By 1954, one out of every two members of the territorial legislature was nisei.

Hawaii enjoyed considerable economic growth in the years following World War II. Not all was satisfactory with the growers, however. There were labor strikes by the sugar cane and pineapple workers. In the meantime, the movement toward statehood continued. Finally, in 1959 Hawaii became the fiftieth state.

Senator Daniel Innoye is one of Hawaii's two United States senators.

Since gaining statehood, Hawaii has changed tremendously. Hawaii's population and economy have grown steadily. Sugar and pineapple growing, although still important, no longer dominate the economy. Tourism has become the major industry, bringing in more than six million people a year to the islands. New resorts were built on Hawaii, Kauai, Maui, and Molokai in the 1970s. Presently, Hawaiians are looking for creative ways to continue the tourism industry while also preserving the environment.

The island paradise of the Polynesians has gone through many difficult changes. Now it has its place in the modern world as a state, as an ethnic melting pot, as an increasingly varied economy, and as an island paradise.

Hawaii's Generous Princess

What if you were given the chance to become a king or queen. Would you say yes? If you did so, what would you do to help your people?

Bernice Pauahi Paki Bishop was the great granddaughter of King Kamehameha I. She could have been queen of Hawaii. In 1872 King Kamehameha V lay dying. He had no wife or children. Who would rule his people after he was gone? Kamehameha V called Princess Bernice Bishop to his side. He asked Bernice to wear the crown. He said it would be best for Hawaii's people. She politely said, "No, no, not me. I do not need it." Even today, Hawaiians do not know why she chose not to be queen. What they do know is that Bernice Bishop was a great leader. She was generous and caring to her people even without the crown.

Bernice Bishop was born in 1831. Her mother, Konia, was the granddaughter of the great Hawaiian king, Kamehameha I. Her father, Abner Paki, was a Hawaiian high chief. Bernice was educated at the Royal School. She was a very intelligent girl. She excelled in school, especially in music. By age ten, she played the piano very well.

Bernice's parents wished her to marry a member of Hawaii's royal

Bernice Pauahi Paki broke off her engagement to Kamehameha V to marry Charles Bishop.

King Kalakaua is among those pictured here on the grounds of the Iolani Palace. King Kalakaua succeeded to the throne two years after Bernice Bishop refused it.

family. They arranged for her to be married to Kamehameha V, but Bernice went against their plans. She broke off that engagement. In 1850 she married Charles Reed Bishop, a non-Hawaiian. Charles was from New York. He had come to Hawaii as a young man. Through honesty and hard work, he had become very successful in business. He became the head of the only bank in Hawaii. He was also foreign minister for the kingdom. He cared deeply for the Hawaiian people. And he was very much in love with Bernice.

Bernice and Charles were very happy together. They lived for many years in the Paki home in Honolulu. Bernice was an avid gardener of native plants. She collected artifacts of Hawaiian culture. Their house was a cultural center. Much of their attention was focused on the protection of Hawaii's heritage.

The Bishop Museum is also Hawaii's State Museum of Natural and Cultural History. It houses over a million Pacific and Hawaiian cultural objects, as well as millions of insect, plant, and animal specimens.

Charles was active in business and the government. Bernice worked for the education of native Hawaiian children. She knew most Hawaiians never went to school. Only because she was a member of the royal family had she been allowed the opportunity to go to school. She believed the future of the Hawaiian people lay in education. Mrs. Bishop's greatest goal was to build a school for all Hawaiian children. She encouraged Hawaii's leaders to build such a school. When she died in 1884, this had not yet happened.

But Bernice Bishop had made sure her dream would come true. She was the last living member of the Kamehameha family. She was owner of one ninth of all the land in the Hawaiian Islands. In her will, she left all this to benefit her people. She requested that two schools be built. Her husband, Charles, made sure it was so.

As chairman of the Bishop Estates, Charles opened the Kamehameha schools. The school for boys opened in 1887; the school for girls opened seven years later. The two schools overlook downtown Honolulu. They have provided educational opportunities for thousands of native Hawaiians.

But Charles Reed Bishop did not stop with the founding of the schools. He knew Princess Bishop's dream for Hawaiians was larger than that. In 1889 he founded the Bishop Museum on Bernice Street in Honolulu. He wanted a world-class museum to house Bernice's collection of Hawaiian artifacts. He believed the museum would ensure that his wife's memory lived on.

Today, the Bishop Museum is considered the principal museum of the Pacific. It is the world's center for Hawaiian and Polynesian artifacts. Its mission is to serve and advise Hawaii's multicultural community. The Bishop Museum is associated with Yale University and the University of Hawaii. Anyone seeking to understand Hawaii's native culture would begin their research at the Bishop Museum.

The museum also publishes books. The Bishop Museum Press, founded in 1892, is the oldest book publisher in Hawaii. It has more than five hundred titles in print. It is the leading publisher of books about the Pacific peoples.

Bernice Pauahi Paki Bishop did not choose to be queen of Hawaii. But because of her love for the Hawaiian people, Hawaii is richer today. Her generosity has ensured Hawaiians international respect and recognition. Even without the crown, Bernice Bishop remains one of Hawaii's greatest leaders.

This artifact from the Bishop Museum is a representation of the head of the war god Kukailimoku. The framework is a wicker basket covered with netting.

Agriculture, Aquaculture, and Lots of Aloha

When you think of Hawaii, you probably think of beautiful islands where tourists wear necklaces of orchids, swim near sandy beaches, and eat exotic foods. If so, you're right.

Tourism is Hawaii's leading industry. More than six million people a year come to enjoy the beauty of the islands. They bring about $11 billion a year into the economy. But there's much more to Hawaii's economy than tourists. You might think of sugar and pineapples, but would you think of soldiers? The second-largest source of Hawaii's income is federal defense. The United States Pacific Command is centered in Hawaii. It is responsible for defending United States interests in an area that covers about fifty percent of Earth's surface.

Tourism and government activities are called service industries. They produce services instead of manufactured or agricultural products. Other service industries are a big part of Hawaii's economy, too. They include businesses such as medicine, law, insurance, banking, and real estate.

This helicopter is flying near Kilauea Crater. Kilauea is one of the active volcanoes that tourists can visit.

Service industries have produced the major part of Hawaii's income since the 1950s. Before that, the state's income came mostly from growing sugar cane and pineapples. These are still the two main crops grown on the islands. In fact, Hawaii is the number one pineapple-producing state in the nation. Refined sugar and canned pineapple are the biggest products of the state's manufacturing industry.

Flowers are another important crop. Hilo, on the island of Hawaii, is the center of the industry that grows orchids. It is also a center for flower packaging. Hawaii is the only state in the union that grows coffee. Hawaii grows some other crops that are unique in the United States. These include macadamia nuts, guava, passion fruit, taro, and mangoes.

This United States Navy ship is stationed at Pearl Harbor, one of the United States' most important naval bases.

Hawaii's mild climate means low costs for heating and winter clothing. But the cost of living is still higher than almost all the other states. The main reason is that almost everything people need must be brought in from other states or countries. The cost of transportation must be added to the price people pay for these goods.

Hawaii produces much of the food its citizens need, however. Most of the beef it uses comes from large cattle ranches. Several of these ranches are on the island of Hawaii. Other islands also supply food for local tables. Oahu, for example, has many dairy and egg farms. Maui and Kauai produce cattle and hogs. Hawaiian farmers grow alfalfa, beans, potatoes, and cabbage.

Hawaii is developing technological resources. It now has several satellite tracking and spaceship

communication centers. It is a world leader in astronomy, with nine major telescopes. The state is ideally suited for research into the oceans, too. Private companies as well as government agencies have oceanographic projects underway. Aquaculture is also a growing industry in Hawaii. Aquaculture is the raising of animals and plants that live in water.

Hawaii doesn't depend only on sugar cane and pineapples anymore. Its economy is much more complicated—and much more diverse.

Kona, on the Big Island of Hawaii, is the only part of the state where coffee is grown. Kona coffee is famous for its deep, rich taste.

One of the best spots on Earth for stargazing is the Mauna Kea Observatory because of the unpolluted air, lack of surrounding light, and usually cloudless sky.

In the 1970s and the 1980s, Hawaii began to develop its aquaculture, or fish-farming, industry. These men are harvesting giant freshwater prawns.

Hawaii's native plants are important to the state's economy. However, development and the introduction of nonnative plants have endangered many species.

Downhill All the Way

Hawaii's tourist industry isn't made up only of hotels and restaurants. It also includes many small organizations that offer tours and unique experiences to visitors.

One of the simplest, smoothest, and most delightful tourist attractions in Hawaii always begins with a question—"You ready to go downhill?" For two and a half hours, Bob Kiger and his group of tourists cruise on bicycles from the top of a volcanic mountain to the sea—downhill all the way. "All my life I worked so hard selling things, and here's something I don't have to sell. People just want it. They want as much of it as they can get. They want to go downhill," Bob said.

Somehow, it seems like a very Hawaiian thing to do. Or at any rate, it is the sort of thing for which people go to Hawaii.

"The first time I rode a bike was nothing like this," Bob said. "This is a cruise. I mean, look, effortless. What could be more visual than cruising through this eucalyptus forest right here? Smelling it. Smell it! Just fantastic. Like cruising through a tube of mentholatum."

Where but Hawaii could you bicycle downhill through a eucalyptus forest? Most people who come to visit Hawaii want to be far from the hurry and tension of cities. They want to cruise on bicycles down the Haleakala Highway on Maui. They want to relax by going downhill all the way.

Bob Kiger is ready to go downhill.

Bob Kiger says that life is a downhill cruise. People need to give up their fears and "go with it."

The group cruises down Haleakala Highway. They will travel 38 miles in about three hours.

The New from the Old

People affect the land they live on. But the land affects them first. Hawaii's climate is perfect for growing sugar cane. So people learned how to make a living doing that. They built plantations where the work could be done and the workers could live. Often the plantations were owned by families who ran them for generations.

Sugar is not nearly as important to Hawaii as it once was. Many of the old plantations have been closed. Now Hawaii is better for attracting tourists. So people have learned how to make a living from tourism.

"We've been here for one hundred years, and we have ties to the past. We are still a family company,

This house is kept as it was many years ago to give tourists an idea of what living on an old sugar plantation was like.

Mike Fay wants tourists to experience the natural flavor of Hawaii.

and our reasons for development may not be only the dollar. We want to be sure that we do something that's in keeping with what we have here in Waimea, the character of the town." Mike Fay was speaking about the sugar plantation begun by his grandfather. Mike couldn't make a living growing sugar cane on the plantation anymore. But he decided to use it in a different way. He planned to give tourists the opportunity to live for a while on the old plantation.

"We have what's left of a sugar plantation," Mike explained as he got started. "We've got the camp, we've got the old mill building, we've got the shops. We've got the churches on our property. We've got the manager's house. For us to tear all that down and start from scratch will make us look like any other place. We think we can create something that nobody else has."

So the carpenters repaired the sagging porches. The plasterers went to work on the walls. The plumbers put in modern kitchens and bathrooms. It wasn't quite the way it was when the plantation workers lived here. If it were, tourists wouldn't stay. But something of the past was saved, and another Hawaiian family still earns a living from the land that grew sugar.

The Colors of Hawaii

In most places on Earth, human life goes back far beyond history. We can only guess at its hidden origins. But Hawaii is different. Hawaii is a group of volcanic islands in the middle of the Pacific Ocean. The first people who ever lived there came late in the history of humanity.

To the lush green and bright flowers of the islands, the Polynesians brought the color of their own culture. And each group that came after them—Japanese, Chinese, Portuguese, Filipino, Korean, European, American—added another shade. There has been some blending. Each culture has mingled a little on the edges with every other culture. But each color has also kept its brilliance, its own special quality.

Dancing and music, for example, have always been a part of Hawaii. The graceful hula was a way the original Hawaiians prayed and spoke to their gods. But the ukulele, that very Hawaiian instrument, was created from a small guitar brought to the islands by

This festive parade float celebrates Hawaii's history and traditions.

the Portuguese. And the favorite song of Hawaii—"Aloha Oe," which was composed by Queen Liliuokalani—has a beautiful, haunting melody. But it is one that owes more to American popular music than to the traditional music of Hawaii.

The muumuu—a loose, brightly colored dress worn throughout these islands—was introduced by the American missionaries. And even the most traditional of European clothing takes on a special quality in Hawaii.

This woman is making leis, the traditional flower necklace of Hawaii.

Language has its own color in Hawaii, too. English is spoken in Hawaii, but Hawaiian is also an official state language. Its influence shows in the names of the islands, in symbols of the state, and in words you probably recognize like *aloha*, *ukulele*, and *hula*. The Hawaiian language goes back to the Polynesians, who were the first people to arrive on the islands. It is one of several Polynesian languages.

Hawaiian is unusual because it has so few consonants. Its alphabet includes only 12 letters—*a, e, h, i, k, l, m, n, o, p, u,* and *w*. Usually Hawaiian is written with certain phonetic marks that help show how to pronounce it. For example, the mark ' indicates the kind of break between syllables you would make between the *ohs* when you say "oh-oh." In addition, sometimes the vowels are marked with macrons, like this: ā, ē, ī, ō, ū. These marks tell you to accent the syllable in which that vowel appears. Otherwise, the accent in most Hawaiian words is on the next-to-last syllable.

The name of the state is properly written Hawai'i. How does knowing that change the way you pronounce it?

Some other words and phrases include:

aloha	hello, goodbye, love
haku	to make or arrange, as a lei
Hau'oli Makahiki Hou	Happy New Year
hula	dance
kapu	forbidden
kōkua	cooperation
lānai	porch or veranda
lei	necklace made from flowers, leaves, or shells
lū'au	Hawaiian feast
mahalo	thank you
malihini	newcomer, visitor
mu'umu'u	loose dress
'ohana	family
'ono	delicious

In everything from food to religion to language, Hawaii is a bright, colorful mixture for the senses. It is as though the culture of Hawaii tries to match the birds and flowers, the sparkling sand of the beaches, and the deep blue of the ocean.

Dancers perform their native dances for tourists.

Volcanoes National Park

Active volcanoes, a tropical rain forest, and beaches of black sand are just a few of the things to see at Hawaii Volcanoes National Park. It is located on the island of Hawaii—known to Hawaiians as the "Big Island."

Because of its gentle tropical climate, Hawaii is rich in plant life. Many plant species in Hawaii are endemic, meaning they are found nowhere else on Earth. This is because of the isolation of the Hawaiian Islands. After all, the islands are 2,400 miles away from the nearest continent. But many endemic plants that once thrived in Hawaii are now extinct. They were forced out by other plant life that

Hawaii's black sand beaches formed when lava from volcanoes flowed into the ocean. This beach is in Hawaii Volcanoes National Park.

Kilauea Crater has not stopped erupting since 1983. This lava flow is from a dual eruption of Mauna Loa and Kilauea, which occurred March 30, 1984.

was brought into the area. Hawaii Volcanoes National Park was created in 1916 to help preserve the area's unique natural features. Naturalists are still working to preserve the remaining endemic species. They know that the ecosystem at Hawaii Volcanoes National Park is like no other place. It is important to preserve and protect the park for future generations.

If you're curious about volcanoes, this is the place to go. The park covers 377 square miles. It has two active volcanoes—Kilauea and Mauna Loa. Each is special in its own way.

Kilauea is the world's most active volcano. It has erupted 40 times since 1924. Sometimes lava erupts out the top of the mountain. Other times it flows out the side. This is known as a flank eruption. Kilauea has been continuously erupting out of one side since January 3, 1983. Scientists do not know how long this eruption will go on. But it's already set the record for the longest flank eruption in history. In the past 1,100 years, lava from Kilauea has covered more than 500 hundred square miles!

Visitors can hike inside the crater at Kilauea's peak. The smell of sulphur rises from deep within the earth. Steam hisses from cracks in the rocky walls.

Near the edge of the crater is Volcano House. It is the only hotel in the whole park. The hotel includes a fireplace that has been been kept lit for over 120 years. It also has three restaurants. Some dining areas have glass walls so that diners can take in the magnificent views. Just imagine eating your lunch while looking out at an active volcano!

Kilauea is remarkable, but it is tiny compared to Mauna Loa. This mountain is 31,677 feet from its base on the ocean floor to its peak. That is a distance of just about six miles, making it the world's tallest active volcano. But that isn't why Mauna Loa is known as the largest mountain on Earth. Its entire mass takes up 10,000 cubic miles! During the past 1,100 years, Mauna Loa's lava has flowed over 2,000 square miles of the island. During the century, Mauna Loa has erupted 14 times. Its last eruption was in 1984. For a short time during that eruption, lava flows threatened the nearby city of Hilo. These volcanoes can still be dangerous.

At Hawaii Volcanoes National Park, you will find something interesting everywhere you look. On one slope of Kilauea is a tropical rain forest. The annual rainfall here is more than one hundred inches. Visitors can get a close look at plenty of unusual plants and animals.

Many visitors are fascinated by the park's black sand beaches. When lava flows down the mountainside, it meets the ocean, and breaks into tiny black particles. The black sand is carried along the coast and sometimes forms deposits along the shoreline. If the black sand is deposited in an area protected from large waves, beaches can form. These beaches are spectacular to look at. But sooner or later, lava will flow over and cover them. In 1992 lava covered the well-known black sand beach known as Kamoamoa.

The natural riches of Hawaii Volcanoes National Park will thrill visitors for years to come. This is a magical place with smoking mountaintops and lush tropical forests. It is a place visitors will remember throughout a lifetime.

This woman is photographing a spot where lava from Mauna Loa flowed over the road. She is standing on older lava that has cooled and hardened.

Planning the Future

Tourists come to Hawaii because of its climate, its exotic beauty, and its beaches. But tourists also come for its history and culture. Clearly, those things will not change. So tourism will continue to be a major part of Hawaii's future.

Tourism does bring some problems with it, however. Many Hawaiians are unhappy about using their treasured rituals and customs to entertain tourists. The natural beauty that draws tourists to Hawaii is in some ways endangered by them. Every hotel built for tourists takes a little bit away from that beauty. And having so many people in the islands affects the surroundings in other ways. Hawaii has many endangered species. And its fresh water supply is fragile, too.

But Hawaiians are approaching the problems of the future with ingenuity and confidence. They are developing other sources of income and employment. Then Hawaii's economy will not be so dependent on tourism. For example, high technology companies are beginning to locate in Hawaii. Film and television

You're never far from a view of the ocean when you're in Hawaii.

production is a growing business. Others sources of income include ocean research and the development of special foods. Explorations into the raising of plants and animals that live in water has resulted in a growing aquaculture industry. Seafoods, such as fish, oysters, and shrimp, are becoming important "crops."

Hawaiians are also working on energy conservation. Currently, Hawaii imports the petroleum that provides about ninety percent of its energy. Its goal is to be able to produce its own energy by the year 2000. Hawaii is one of the leading states in the development and use of alternate energy sources. For example, the island of Hawaii is developing geothermal power for its own use. The state of Hawaii is using agricultural wastes for generating electricity. It also has more solar water heaters per person than anywhere else in the United States. An interesting source being developed is the power of the wind. Hawaii is one of the few states with commercial "wind farms."

Just as important as the attempts to vary the state's economy are the attempts to preserve the Hawaiian culture. Hawaiians are proud of their traditions. These traditions include a deep respect for the land. The seeds of Hawaii's future may lie in its past. But the future also includes much that is new and exciting.

This small roadside market in Waimea reveals a part of Hawaiian lifestyle not included in tourist brochures.

400 to 900	About this time, Polynesians come from other Pacific Islands and settle Hawaii.
1778	Captain James Cook visits Hawaii on his way from the South Pacific to the northwest coast of America.
1795	King Kamehameha I brings all the islands except Kauai and Niihau together under his rule.
1810	Kauai and Niihau become part of Kamehameha's kingdom.
1819	Kamehameha I dies. His son Kamehameha II takes power.
1820	Protestant missionaries come to the island to convert the Hawaiians to Christianity.
1835	The first permanent sugar plantation is built by Ladd & Company.
1840	Hawaii adopts its first constitution.
1852	Chinese workers begin to arrive to work on the sugar plantations.
1868	Japanese workers immigrate to Hawaii to work on the plantations.
1887	The major landowners and taxpayers force King Kalakaua to approve a new constitution.
1891	Queen Liliuokalani comes to power and begins to fight for political control.
1893	A rebellion backed by the United States ambassador to Hawaii overthrows Queen Liliuokalani.
1894	After President Grover Cleveland refuses to annex Hawaii, the leaders of the rebellion declare Hawaii a republic.
1895	Queen Liliuokalani is arrested after giving up her counterrevolution.
1898	Hawaii becomes a possession of the United States.
1900	The Territory of Hawaii is established.
1911	Pearl Harbor is built.
1927	The first airplane flight is made from the mainland to Hawaii.
1941	Japan stages a surprise attack on Pearl Harbor and Oahu. The United States enters World War II.
1950	The legislature of the Territory of Hawaii approves a constitution that will go into effect at statehood.
1959	Hawaii becomes the fiftieth state.
1960s	The tourist industry begins to boom.
1975	A massive tidal wave and two earthquakes hit Hawaii, causing enormous damage.
1986	John Waihee is the first person of Hawaiian ancestry to be elected governor.
1992	Hurricane Iniki sweeps over Hawaii, killing three people and causing about $1 billion in property damage.

The flag has eight stripes, representing the main Hawaiian Islands. The red, white, and blue colors in the upper left-hand corner resemble the British Union Jack, from which the flag was designed.

Hawaii Almanac

Nickname. The Aloha State

Capital. Honolulu

State Bird. Nene (Hawaiian goose)

State Flower. Yellow hibiscus

State Tree. Kukui

State Motto. *Ua mau ke ea o ka aina i ka pono* (The Life of the Land Is Perpetuated in Righteousness)

State Song. "Hawaii Ponoi"

Abbreviations. Ha. (traditional); HI (postal)

Statehood. August 21, 1959, the 50th state

Government. Congress: U.S. senators, 2; U.S. representatives, 2. State Legislature: senators, 25; representatives, 51. Counties: 5

Area. 6,459 sq mi (16,729 sq km), 47th in size among the states

Greatest Distances. north/south, 230 mi (370 km); east/west, 350 mi (565 km). Coastline: 750 mi (1,207 km)

Elevation. Highest: Mauna Kea, 13,796 ft (4,205 m). Lowest: sea level, along the coast

Population. 1990 Census: 1,115,274 (16% increase over 1980), 40th in population among the states. Density: 173 persons per sq mi (67 persons per sq km). Distribution: 89% urban, 11% rural. 1980 Census: 964,691

Economy. *Agriculture:* sugar cane, pineapples, beef cattle, flowers, coffee, macadamia nuts, avocados, bananas. *Fishing:* yellowfin and skipjack tuna. *Manufacturing:* food processing, printed materials, clothing, petroleum products, concrete. *Mining:* crushed stone

State Seal

State Flower: Yellow hibiscus

State Bird: Nene (Hawaiian goose)

Annual Events

★ Hula Bowl football game in Honolulu (January)

★ Hawaiian Open International Golf Tournament on Oahu (January/February)

★ Merrie Monarch Hula Festival in Hilo (April)

★ Lei Day, statewide (May)

★ Fiftieth State Fair on Oahu (May/June)

★ International Festival of the Pacific in Hilo (July)

★ Aloha Festivals, statewide (September/October)

★ World Cup of Surfing on Oahu (November/December)

Places to Visit

★ Aloha Tower in Honolulu

★ Barking Sands on Kauai

★ Hawaii Volcanoes National Park on Hawaii

★ Kaimu Black Sand Beach on Hawaii

★ Kapiolani Park, near Honolulu

★ Kula Botanical Garden on Maui

★ Mauna Loa Macadamia Nut Factory on Hawaii

★ Nuuanu Pali on Oahu

★ Pearl Harbor on Oahu

★ Polynesian Cultural Center on Oahu

★ Sea Life Park on Oahu

★ Waimea Canyon on Kauai

Index